ON THE FRONT LINE
Guerrilla Poems
of El Salvador

ON THE FRONT LINE
Guerrilla Poems
of El Salvador

editado y traducido por
edited and translated by

Claribel Alegría and
Darwin J. Flakoll

CURBSTONE PRESS

Second Printing: 1996; Third Printing: 2002

This publication was supported in part by donations, and
by grants from The Connecticut Commission On The Arts,
a state arts agency whose funds are recommended by the Governor
and appropriated by the State Legislature

cover design: Barbara Byers

ISBN: 0-915306-86-7
LC: 89-62126

published by
CURBSTONE PRESS, 321 Jackson St., Willimantic, CT 06226
phone: (203) 423-5110   info@curbstone.org   www.curbstone.org

CONTENTS

INTRODUCTION

"When history can no longer be written with pens, it must be written with rifles."

The above phrase is attributed to Farabundo Martí, who met his death before a firing squad at the outbreak of the peasant insurrection in El Salvador in 1932. That disorganized uprising was crushed with the slaughter of 30,000 peasants, and it was followed by 50 years of military dictatorships which succeeded each other in power by means of coup d'etats or fraudulent elections.

Another wave of revolutionary discontent began to swell in the early 1970s with the appearance of the first politico-military organizations, all sharing the conviction that, since peaceful democratic change was clearly barred in El Salvador, the country's future history "must be written with rifles."

Today, nearly two decades and 60,000 violent deaths later, this tiny Central American country is immersed in a full-scale civil war. The Farabundo Martí National Liberation Front (Frente Farabundo Martí de Liberacion Nacional — FMLN) controls nearly one third of the national territory, divided into several major fighting fronts and controlled zones, and its guerrilla columns have held the Salvadoran army in check for the past seven years, despite the torrent of military and economic aid and counter-insurgency advice poured into the country by the government of the United States.

This book is a collection of poems by Salvadoran revolutionists on the different fighting fronts of the FMLN who have from time to time put aside their rifles and taken up the pen to express the feelings evoked by the cruel, bloody struggle in which they are engaged. Some of them have fallen in the course of the struggle. Others were established poets before they took up arms in the revolutionary cause. But the majority of them "came to poetry by way of revolution," in Roque Dalton's phrase, and were first given an opportunity to be heard by reciting their verses (transcribed in cassettes) over Radio Farabundo Martí, one of the clandestine radio transmitters maintained by the FMLN in the guerrilla-controlled zone of Chaletenango.

This anthology does not pretend to be exhaustive, though the compilers made an effort to seek as wide and representative a selection as was possible within the harsh limitations imposed by war. Roque Dalton, perhaps the exemplary poet-revolutionary of the Salvadoran struggle, is not represented here since his work has been so widely published in Latin America, Europe and the United States (see Poems by Roque Dalton, Curbstone Press, 1984).

Roque, who died in 1975 on the eve of his 40th birthday, was one of the first poets to fall. Delfi Góychez Fernández was 20 years old in May 1979 when she was killed a few weeks after finishing the poem here included. She received two police bullets in the back while delivering provisions to compañeros of the FMLN who had occupied the Venezuelan Embassy in San Salvador. Jaime Suárez Quemain was 30, the editor of an independent newspaper, when he and a companion were arrested by plainclothes men in a San Salvador cafe in 1980. Their mutilated bodies were discovered the following day. Roberto Saballos was assassinated by a death squad the same year, and José María Cuéllar was gunned down by unknown persons on a street in San Salvador in 1981. So far as is known at this writing, the remaining poets included in this volume are still alive, still wielding their rifles and pens in the combat zones of El Salvador in a collective effort to forge a new history and a new culture in that war-ravaged land.

— The editors
Managua, 1989

On The Front Line

UNA HISTORIA

A mi hermana María Teresa Saballos, desaparecida por
la Guardia Nacional el 15 de septiembre de 1979.

Esta es la historia de María Teresa
de sus días cansados
y sus noches largas
de su madre sola
y su hijo joven
esta es la historia de su hastío
de su andar pausado
y su pelo negro
su sonrisa franca
y sus manos viejas.

Esta es su historia
con más dolores que alegrías
con menos años que tristezas.
Esta es la historia de su adiós
de su despedida sin despedidas.

Esta es la historia de su madre
de sus pasos perdidos
de su suave espera de cárcel en cárcel
de tribunal en tribunal
con sonrisas de jueces
de manos vacías.

Esta es la historia de sus ojos
que buscan su pelo
su mirada clara
y sus manos fuertes

A STORY

For my sister, María Teresa Saballos, disappeared by the
National Guard on September 15, 1979.

This is the story of María Teresa
of her weary days
and her long nights
of her lone mother
and her young son
this is the story of her boredom
of her slow steps
and her black hair
her open smile
and her old-woman's hands.

This is her story
with more grief than happiness
with fewer years than sadnesses.
This is the story of her goodbye
of her farewell without farewells.

This is the story of her mother
of her useless steps
of her quiet waiting from jail to jail
from court to court
with smiling judges
who are empty-handed.

This is the story of her eyes
that peer at her hair
her clear gaze
and her strong hands

que se perdieron hace tiempo
en la fría madrugada
esta es la historia de María Teresa
esta es la historia de mi pueblo.

— Roberto Saballos

that were lost long ago
in the cold dawn
this is the story of María Teresa
this is the story of my people.

— Roberto Saballos

A VOS

Ey compa.
Sí, a vos te hablo
a vos que no sabés leer y escribir
te invito a que abramos juntos
la puerta que por tantos años
se ha mantenido cerrada para vos
y salgás de ese cuarto
de ignorancia y ceguera
para aprender y enseñar tu realidad.

Has caminado un largo camino,
lo sé, pero si aprendés a leer y escribir
habrás caminado la mayor parte del camino
pues, mientras más aprendés
será más grande la derrota del enemigo.
No, no sintás pena ni vergüenza,
al contrario sentite orgulloso
de poder librar y ganar
contra el analfabetísmo
dentro del proceso de la
guerra popular revolucionaria.

— Carmela, alfabetizadora del FMLN

TO YOU

Hey, compa.
Yes, I'm talking to you
to you who don't know how to read and write
I invite you to open with me
the door that for so many years
has been closed to you
and move out of that room
of ignorance and blindness
to learn and teach your reality.

You've walked a long road, I know,
but if you learn to read and write
you'll have walked the longest part of the road
because the more you learn
the greater will be the enemy's defeat
no, don't feel sorry or ashamed
on the contrary, feel proud
to free yourself and win out
against illiteracy
in the process of the
popular revolutionary war.

— Carmela, literacy teacher of the FMLN

USTED

Usted
amado compañero
se fue desdibujando
en el horizonte.

El sol se fue apagando cayó la noche
y qué frío
tranquilidad apacible
noche estrellada
hoy añoro
aquella playita, ¿se acuerda?

— Ruth, educadora política

YOU

You
beloved companion
faded away
on the horizon.

The sun went out, night fell
and it's chilly
peaceful tranquility
a starry night
now I long for
that small beach, remember?

— Ruth, political educator

A VOS QUE TE FUISTE AL FRENTE

Tenía 19 años,
y una estrella en el puño de la mano,
tus recortes de beisbol
en la pared del cuarto,
cassettes de Barry Manilow y Pablo Milanés
y además la foto de una chavala
en la billetera gastada:
uno de tus mayores tesoros clandestinos.

El otro fue insomnio,
un pensamiento que fue creciendo
hasta envolverte,
la decisión que encontraste
en el rostro de tu madre,
en el frescor de la tarde,
respirando con todo tu cuerpo, aún adolescente,
en los chavalitos de la barriada,
llenos de polvo y alegría,
y allí estás ahora,
muralla,
trinchera inamovible,
posta nocturna,
vigila permanente bajo bandera de Sandino,
avanzando definitivamente
sobre las hienas podridas de Pastora,
sobre los parias dirigidos por la CIA
defendiendo la estrella que conserva con tanto celo,
en el puño de la mano,
en el compartimiento especial de la mochila,
en esa foto de la billetera gastada.

— Anónimo

FOR YOU WHO WENT TO THE FRONT

You were nineteen
with a star clutched in your fist,
your baseball clippings
pinned in your room,
cassettes of Barry Manilow and Pablo Milanes,
and the photo of a girl
in your battered billfold:
one of your greatest clandestine treasures.

The other was an insomnia,
a thought that kept growing
until it enveloped you,
the decision you found
in your mother's features,
in the cool of the evening,
breathing with your whole still-adolescent body
among the neighborhood kids,
smeared with dirt and happiness,
and there you are now,
wall,
unmovable trench,
nocturnal sentinel,
permanently vigilant under Sandino's flag,
advancing definitively
against Pastora's rotten hyenas,
against the pariahs led by the CIA,
jealously defending the star
you clutch in your hand,
in the special compartment of your knapsack,
in that photo in your battered billfold.

— Anonymous

A LA SOMBRA DE
UNA MUCHACHA EN FLOR

Un poeta asegura que Lil abre las puertas del día
          para que entremos todos,
su poesía es como la amplia masa del pueblo: creadora;
cuando ella sueña un ángel baja sus ojos
y cuando los niños lloran Lil reparte su sonrisa
          la luz y el mundo entero.
Ella escribe libertad desde la oscura cárcel
todo lo ve y lo palpa en el silencio como una niña
los pobres bebemos sus arroyos su exilio de esta vida
          usurpada a sangre y fuego
aprendimos a amarla guerreando
y es el alba afincada en nuestros pechos . . .

— Alfonso Hernández

SHADOWED BY
A BLOSSOMING GIRL

A poet says that Lil opens the daytime doors
            so we all may enter,
her poetry is like the people: creative,
when she dreams an angel lowers his eyes
and when children cry Lil shares her smile
            the light and the whole world.
She writes freedom from the dark cell
she sees everything and touches it silently like a child
we poor drink from her bounty, her exile from this life
            usurped by blood and fire
we learn to love her in each skirmish
she is the perennial daybreak in our hearts.

— Alfonso Hernández

AL AMOR

Quiero escribir a la paz
y lo estamos haciendo.
Construirla es mucho más difícil
pero se puede y debe hacerlo
en mucho de ese decir
y de este vaivén
de hacer y deshacer
de golpe a golpe
de paso a paso
ni un paso hacia atrás
sólo pasos hacia adelante
inclaudicable faena
estoy escribiendo y construyendo
caminando y caminando
escribir toda la vida
y no sólo un instante
aunque mi vida sólo sea un instante
porque el RAN esta encima de nosotros
con mi vida te escribiré
y la historia será escrita
aunque el RAN y el C-47 estén encima
RAN hijueputa y apagué la candela.

— Niño, teniente de una unidad de aseguramiento

TO LOVE

I want to write a letter to peace
and we are doing that.
To construct it is much more difficult
but it can and must be done
amidst the talking
and this to and fro
of doing and undoing
of blow after blow
and step after step
not a single step backward
only steps forward
unwavering toil
I am writing and building
walking and walking
writing all my life
not only an instant
though my life may only last an instant
because the RAN* is overhead.
I'll write you with my life
and the story will be written
despite the RAN and the C-47 overhead
that bastardly RAN and I blew out the candle.

— Niño, lieutenant of a security unit

*RAN stands for Nocturnal Aerial Reconnaissance, and it's usually a Hercules and a C-47 armed with three 20mm .72 calibre canons just behind the Hercules, with those damned machine guns indiscriminately blasting humanity and life and peace itself.

CON GUSTO MORIRÉ

a mí me van a matar.
cuándo?
no sé . . .
lo que sí tengo claro es que moriré
así, asesinada por el enemigo.

como quiero seguir luchando
siempre estaré luchando para morir así.

como quiero morir junto al pueblo
nunca me separaré de él.
como es nuestro grito el que llegará
deberé gritarlo siempre.

como el futuro y la historia
están con nosotros,
jamás me desviaré del camino.

como aspiro a ser revolucionaria
mis puntos de vista
y todas mis aspiraciones
estarán a partir de ello.

no tendré miedo nunca.
todo lo que haga
tiene que ser un golpe para el enemigo,
en cualquier forma que se dé.

siempre estaré activa.

lo que sí es seguro

es que me van a matar.

I'LL DIE GLADLY

they're going to kill me
when?
I don't know . . .
what I do know clearly is that I'll die
that way, assassinated by the enemy.

since I long to go on fighting
I'll always keep fighting to die that way.

since I want to die with the people
I'll never be separated from them.
since it's our shout that reaches out
I have to keep shouting forever.

since the future and history
are with us,
I'll never stray from the road.

since I aspire to be a revolutionary
my viewpoints
and all my hopes
depart from that.

I'll never be afraid.
everything I do
must be a blow against the enemy,
however I give it.

I'll always be active

what is really certain

is that they're going to kill me.

y mi sangre regará nuestra tierra
y crecerán las flores de la libertad

y el futuro abrirá sus brazos
y caluroso, lleno de amor,

nos acogerá en su pecho nuestra madre
nuestra patria
reirá felíz al estar de nuevo con su hijo
con su pueblo
con el niño que ayer lloraba un pedazo de pan
y que hoy
crece como río.

con la madre que moría lentamente
y hoy vive su lejano sueño de ayer.

con el eterno combatiente
cuya sangre
alimentó el día
que algún día llegará.

sí, con gusto moriré, llena de amor,
quiero morir de la manera más natural en estos tiempos
y en mi país:
asesinada por el enemigo de mi pueblo.

> — Delfy Góchez Fernández
> (Santa Tecla, 10 de mayo de 1979)

and my blood will water our land
and the flowers of freedom will grow

and the future will open its arms
and tenderly, filled with love,

our mother, our fatherland,
will press us to its breast
will laugh happily to be once more with its child,
with its people
with the child that yesterday wept for a crust of bread
and who today
grows like a river.

with the mother who died slowly
and today lives her far-off dream of yesterday.

with the eternal combatant
whose blood
nourished the day
that some day will arrive.

yes, I'll die happily, filled with love,
I want to die in the most natural way in these times
and in my country:
assassinated by the enemy of my people.

> — Delfy Góchez Fernández
> (Santa Tecla, May 10, 1979)

HIJOS DE AMERICA

A Horacio heróico.

América te amo
y no canto a tus volcanes
vivo con alegría
tu madrugada clandestina
conozco los muros de los cuarteles
la risa de los esbirros
y no me asustan
los batallones especiales
que sueñan con despedazar
tus heróicas guerrillas
en esta hora
de espadas y tempestades
América te amo
y voy por los montes
mil veces orgulloso
de ser tu hijo.

— Jacobo, capitán de un destacamento guerrillero

SONS OF AMERICA

For heroic Horatio.

America I love you
and I don't sing to your volcanos
I live joyfully
your clandestine early dawn
I know the fortress walls
the laughter of the mad dogs
and they don't scare me
nor the special battalions
that dream of chopping up
your heroic guerrillas
in this hour of swords and tempests
America I love you
and I move among the mountains
prouder than ever
to be your son.

— Jacobo, captain of a guerrilla detachment

9 DE NOVIEMBRE

A Justo Mejía.

Aquel amanecer, Tío Justo,
los paracaidístas
empezaron a morir en las maicilleras
el verano asomaba lentamente
a la orilla de la balacera
dibujando la sombra invencible
de los guerreros descalzos
los mismos cipotes bravos
que sacudieron Cinquera,
El Paraíso, Cerrón Grande,
con su ración operativa
de harina de alegría y ternura
se atrincheraban en secreto
para soportar las cargas del cielo
partiendo la tierra en mil pedazos.

De pronto,
en medio de la arboleda
y del estruendo de los Dragones
una mancha de helicópteros
se tendió por los sanjones
para iniciar el segundo desembarco.
De todos los sitios
escogieron el más seguro
de frente a la .50
mejor conocida como "Victoria"
que vino a esperarlos a toda prisa
rascando tierra para empezar a repartir
el plomo justiciero
en el pecho de los esbirros.

NOVEMBER 9th

For Justo Mejía.

That dawn, uncle Justo,
the paratroopers started dying
in the cornfields
summer rose slowly
at the edge of the firefight
sketching the invincible shadows
of the barefoot warriors,
the same daring kids
who shook Cinquera,
El Paraíso, Cerrón Grande,
with their operational rations
of cornmeal, joy and tenderness
they dug trenches secretly
to withstand discharges from the sky
that shattered the earth in a thousand bits.

Suddenly
amidst the trees
and the roar of Dragonflies
a stain of helicopters
spread out across the trenches
to start the second landing.
Of all places they chose the most secure
facing the .50 calibre
— the one we named "Victoria" —
that we rapidly moved up to await them,
dragging it along the ground
so it might mete out
leaden slugs of justice
in the breasts of the wolfpack.

Después de la cortina de tritonal
y antes que los escombros cayeran a tierra
una lluvia de candiles
surcó el viento frío de la mañana,
se sacudieron los Zacatales
y los paracaidístas empezaron
a morir en las maicilleras.

— Jacobo, capitán de un destacamento guerrillero

After the tritonal curtain
and before the rubble struck the earth
a rain of tracers
pierced the chill wind of morning
shook the pastures
and the paratroopers started dying
in the cornfields.

           — Jacobo, captain of a guerrilla detachment

¿QUE ES POESIA?

Poesía es amor por la tradición, por la cicatriz, es romperse
                                        la nariz con
la burguesía nacional reacia y rancia y que para cuando
                                        vengan encima
las autoridades tengan agua las fuentes
y la sangre corra y no os asustéis porque estais prevenidos.
Poesía es reirse de los censores de Claudia Lars, es
                                        intranquilidad,
quillas de pescadores, es la oración del hombre al
                                        hombre no se escapa
nadie. Al que la hizo debeis condenar o perseguirlo,
                                        es responsable ante
la humanidad que ama. Poesía en estos tiempos es para que
                                        te rompan el cráneo.
Hoy quieres pan, luego vas a pedir poesía.
        Poesía es subversión, es un árbol con sus raíces
                                        desintegrando la piedra.

                            — Eduardo Sancho Castañeda
                            (Comandante Fermán Cienfuegos)

WHAT IS POETRY?

Poetry is love of tradition, of the scar, it's breaking
                              your nose against
the stubborn, rancid national bourgeoisie and when the
                              authorities
pull a raid your water tanks are filled
and blood flows and you don't panic because you were ready.
Poetry is to laugh at Claudia Lars' censors, it's
                              restlessness,
it's the fisherman's keel, it's the prayer of man to man
                              that no one escapes.
Whoever makes a poem must be condemned and persecuted,
                              he is responsible before
the humanity he loves. Poetry these days is to break your skull.
Today you want bread, later you'll ask for poetry.
Poetry is subversion, it's a tree whose roots gnaw away
                              at the rock.

                    — Eduardo Sancho Castañeda
                    (Comandante Fermán Cienfuegos)

SIEMPRE TUVE...

Siempre tuve al acecho un fusil,
el tilín, tilín de mi vida fue la gesta morazánica
el niño que durmió en la cueva del tacuazín
devoré los 7 pecados capitales
apunté con el piquito de una tortolita a una ramita seca,
mi vida que siempre la recorrí por la línea dura
los grandes pacifistas acechaban con un abanico multicolor,
olorosos a Old Spice
con moños blanquísimos
chachalaquiando con sus huesos roídos
con sotanas hediondas al baúl de mi abuelita
yo con mi guadaña
yo con mi fusil y su luz ...

> — Eduardo Sancho Castañeda
> (Comandante Fermán Cienfuegos)

I ALWAYS HAD . . .

I always had a rifle at the ready,
the clanging bell of my life was Morazán's epic.
The boy who slept in the tacuazín's cafe
I devoured the seven deadly sins
aimed a turtledove's beak at a dry branch
I always took a hard line with my life
the great pacifists peered over their multi-colored fans,
smelling of Old Spice
with their powdered chignons
clattering their gnawed bones
their cassocks stinking like my grandmother's hope chest
and I with my scythe
I with my rifle and its sparkle . . .

— Eduardo Sancho Castañeda
(Comandante Fermán Cienfuegos)

COMPA GUERRILLERA

Muchacha guerrillera de mi pueblo.
Qué hermosa luces en nuestras columnas
eres luz y fortaleza en nuestro accionar
muchacha guerrillera de mi pueblo
que hermosa luces con tu fusil al hombro
hermosa como los atardeceres en los cerros
o en un brillante atardecer en Guazapa.

Compa guerrillera de mi pueblo
ejemplo en todo momento
aún en esos de desaliento tantos
dulzura es tu presencia en tantos momentos.

Muchacha guerrillera de mi pueblo
estás aquí, allá, en todo lugar,
en la cocina, en la clínica,
en las montañas, en las compañías.

Aquí y allá eres madre,
portadora de alegrías,
confianza y valentía.

— Julio, combatiente guerrillero

COMPA GUERRILLERA

Guerrilla girl of my people.
You look lovely in our columns
you are light and strength in our actions
guerrilla girl of my people.
You're lovely with your rifle slung on your shoulder
lovely as the mountain evenings
or a brilliant sunset in Guazapa.

Compa guerrillera of my people
always an example
even in those discouraging moments
your presence is always a sweetness

Guerrilla girl of my people
you're here, there, everywhere,
in the kitchen, in the clinic,
in the mountains, in the companies.

Here and there you're the mother
bearer of happiness
confidence and valor.

— Julio, guerrilla combatant

HOY ESTOY AQUI

Yo hacía toallas,
traca, traca, traca,
la lanzadera traca, traca,
derecha a izquierda traca, traca,
hilo va, hilo viene y en la tela se detiene
Yo hacía toallas
sin pago del 7º
cuando llegaba tarde dos minutos
sin derecho a huelga,
a grito, a sindicato
prohibido terminantemente
por la "Constitución Política",
pero un día nos llegaron
como ventarrón las ideas clandestinas
y florecieron letras rojas en las paredes de la fábrica,
"Viva la clase obrera",
y salimos a la calle
y corrimos entre humo de los gases lacrimógenos,
hoy estoy aquí,
fuerza especial del coraje,
explosivo de ira,
en la marcha colectiva,
asaltando, trecho a trecho,
      La Victoria.

— Julio

NOW I'M HERE

I used to make towels,
traca, traca, traca,
the shuttle traca, traca,
right to left, traca, traca,
the thread comes and goes
and stays in the cloth
I used to make towels
without extra pay on Sunday
whenever I arrived two minutes late
with no right to strike,
to protest, to join a union
was flatly prohibited
by the "Political Constitution,"
but one day we received
like a gust of wind clandestine ideas
and red letters flowered on the factory walls,
"Long live the working class,"
and we took to the streets
and ran through a haze of tear gas
now I'm here,
in the Special Force of toughness,
explosive with rage,
in the collective march,
assaulting bit by bit
The Victory.

— Julio

POEMA

Centinela de los cerros
hilando nuestros esfuerzos
mientras triunfamos

cuando regresas tu sonrisa
de oreja a oreja
es nuestro venceremos
es que tú

guerrillero

sos la línea de fuego
de lo que todos hacemos.

— Haydé, alfabetizadora

POEM

Sentinel of the hills
weaving together our efforts
until we triumph

when you return, your
smile from ear to ear
is our guarantee of victory
because you

warrior

are the firing line
of everything we do.

— Haydé, literacy teacher

SI LA MUERTE . . .

Si la muerte viene y pregunta por mí
haga el favor
de decirle que vuelva mañana
que todavía no he cancelado mis deudas
ni he terminado un poema
ni me he despedido de nadie
ni he ordenado mi ropa para el viaje
ni he llevado a su destino el encargo ajeno
ni he echado llave en mis gavetas
ni he dicho lo que debía decir a los amigos
ni he sentido el olor de la rosa que no ha nacido
ni he desenterrado mis raíces
ni he escrito una carta pendiente
que ni siquiera me he lavado las manos
ni he conocido un hijo
ni he empredido caminatas en países desconocidos
ni conozco los siete velos del mar
ni la canción del marino
Si la muerte viniera
diga por favor que estoy entendido
y que me haga una espera
que no he dado a mi novia ni un beso de despedida
que no he repartido mi mano con las de mi familia
ni he desempolvado los libros
ni he silbado la canción preferida
ni me he reconciliado con los enemigos
dígale que no he probado el suicidio
ni he visto libre a mi gente
dígale si viene que vuelva mañana
que no es que le tema pero ni siquiera
he empezado a andar el camino.

— Miguel Huezo Mixco

IF DEATH . . .

If death should come asking for me
do me the favor
of telling him to come back tomorrow
because I still haven't paid my debts
nor finished a poem
nor said goodbye to anyone
nor prepared clothing for the trip
nor delivered that package I promised to
nor locked up my desk drawers
nor told my friends what I should have
nor sniffed the fragrance of the unborn rose
nor laid bare my roots
nor answered an overdue letter
because I haven't even washed my hands
or known a son
or gone hiking in unknown countries
nor do I know the sea's seven sails
nor the song of mariners
If death should come
please tell him I understand
and to wait a bit
because I haven't kissed my sweetheart goodbye
nor shaken hands with my family
nor dusted my books
nor whistled my favorite song
nor become reconciled with my enemies
tell him I haven't yet attempted suicide
nor seen my people freed
tell him if he comes to return tomorrow
that it's not because I fear him but because
I haven't even set off along the road.

— Miguel Huezo Mixco

PARA QUE LO ENTIENDAS
DE UNA VEZ

Porque escribir es también estar contigo
y con la patria
junto a los monumentos
y las urgencias de pan y de amor
escribir no es irse caminando
es salvarse y salvarte
llevarte conmigo a la patria que le cierras
los ojos
y porque escribir es eso
es duro todo lo demás:
que se cierren puertas
y se nieguen manos
para forjar de otro modo este hierro
Porque la patria no está solo en casa
porque tú la buscas donde sabes
que no verás su cuerpo sangrado
Porque escribir no es salir volando
ni apagar las luces
es amar y perdonar redimir y condenar
buscar en todas las partes
romperse el corazón contra el tuyo
y así roto no esperar tranquilamente el futuro
sino irse a encender nuevos fuegos
Porque escribir es amarte y hacer con todos la guerra.

— Miguel Huezo Mixco

SO YOU UNDERSTAND ONCE
AND FOR ALL

Because to write is also to be with you
and with the homeland
along with the monuments
and the urgencies of bread and love
to write is not to go for a stroll
it's to save myself and to save you
to take you with me to the homeland you close
your eyes to
and because writing is all this
everything else is difficult:
that doors are closed
and help denied
to forge this iron in a different way
Because the homeland isn't just a home
because you seek it where you know
you won't see its bleeding body
Because to write is not to run away
nor to turn off the lights
it is to love to pardon to redeem and condemn
to search everywhere
to break my heart against yours
and when broken not to tranquilly await the future
but to go out and light new fires
Because to write is to love you and to fight alongside the rest.

— Miguel Huezo Mixco

HERENCIA

Para D.

He dejado abierta la ventana
para que vengan los hambrientos y los "D" enérgicos
y he dejado mi fusil cargado y listo
para que lo empuñen los albañiles.

En los cimientos de esta casa
encontrarán el metal colado
en los hornos de estos años terribles
no hay nada bajo llave
ni hay gavetas;
he dejado encima los papeles
con bromas de insolente ternura.

También hay una linterna y en el mapa
están marcados los caminos
hasta donde me llevó mi pueblo.
He dejado los cigarros y los fósforos
protegidos de la humedad del tiempo.

La navaja está afilada como una lengua
y hay sal en un rincón cerca de la mesa
ahí están arrugados mis zapatos, viejos zorros,
al pie de la escalera
en el sitio donde pega el primer sol de la mañana
a través de mi ventana.

— Haroldo, propagandista del FMLN

BEQUEATHMENT

For D.

I have the window open
so the famished energetic "D's" can enter
and I've left my rifle loaded and ready
for the construction crew to pick up.

In the foundations of the house
they will find the battered slugs
in the crucible of these awful years
nothing is under lock and key
there are no drawers
I have left my papers on top
with their insolent, tender jests

There's also a flashlight and on the map
are traced the roads
along which my people led me.
I have left the cigarettes and matches
protected from time's humidity.

The razor is sharp as a tongue
and there's salt in a corner near the table.
There are my crumpled shoes, wily foxes,
at the foot of the stairway
where the first morning sun strikes
through my window.

— Haroldo, FMLN propagandist

COMPAÑERA

He escuchado un ruidito
detrás de la choza
y pensé que eras vos la que venía
con tu mundo a cuestas
dando pasos cortos y ligeritos.

Hay serpientes en el campamento
que se deslizan en las trincheras
en el invierno también repican
rumorosas en la hojarasca.
Hay cuzucos que escarban
los hormigueros.
El vientecillo del norte estremece
los chiriviscos.

Tenés que volver a este charral
y contarme las voces
en la línea de fuego
de los hombres que sueñan.

Grandes pelotas de aires y fierro
no pueden tocarte.
Proyectiles de fuego, balas trazadoras,
agujas de frío en este invierno en Cuzcatlán
hojas de acero de la noche chalateca
no podrán tocarte.

— Haroldo

COMPAÑERA

I heard a sound
behind the hut
and I thought it must be you
coming with your world on your shoulders
coming with short, quick footsteps.

There are snakes in the camp
that squirm through the trenches
in the winter their warning rattle
buzzes in the underbrush.
There are cuzucos that delve
into antheaps.
The north wind
makes the branches tremble.

Come back to this bush clump
and tell me of the voices
on the firing line
of the men who are dreaming.

Great gusts of air and metal
cannot touch you.
Fireballs, tracer bullets,
chill needles in the Cuzcatlán winter
steel needles in the Chalateca night
cannot touch you.

— Haroldo

POEMA

Dentro de montañas de esperanza
mares tormentosos
fusiles clamorosos,
van con alas extendidas
atravesando nubes
chorriadas de recuerdos.
Son los muchachos,
es la guerrilla,
con mochilas improvisadas
sin uniforme
con flores en sus ojos
y juventud de lucha
avanzan al combate victorioso
en verano o invierno
soplan fuerte
moviendo nuevas estrellas
en cielos de futuro
son agua clara corriendo
al encuentro de sus mares
soles de mediodia
en desiertos silenciosos
cañones penetrando
el atalaya enemiga.

— Alvaro

POEM

Amidst hope-filled mountains
storm-tossed seas
clamorous rifles
they fly on widespread wings
cutting through clouds
that drip with memories.
They are the lads,
the guerrillas,
with improvised knapsacks
un-uniformed
with flowers in their eyes
and a youth filled with struggle
they advance toward victorious combat
in winter or summer
they breathe strongly
moving new stars
through future skies
they are clear water flowing
to meet new seas
midday suns
in silent deserts
gunbarrels penetrating
the enemy watchtower.

— Alvaro

ALFABETIZAR

Alfabetizábamos con nuestras botas
requisadas y nuestros fusiles
así aprendimos la palabra "enemigo"

Alfabetizábamos con la convivencia
revolucionaria
compartiendo todo en plena lipidia
así aprendimos la palabra "compañero"

Alfabetizábamos con maestras silenciosas
y pigiadas
por quebradas, senderos, caminos y veredas.
Así aprendimos la palabra: "GUINDA"*

Hoy 14 de agosto de 1984 alfabetizamos
ya con lápiz y cartilla.
Y aprenderemos todas las palabras
que hasta ahora llevamos
en el corazón: "Victoria", "Amor."

— Karla, sanitaria y alfabetizadora

TO ALPHABETIZE

We taught the alphabet with our
requisitioned boots and our rifles
and thus we learned the word "enemy."

We taught the alphabet with
revolutionary togetherness
sharing everything when there was nothing
thus we learned the word "companion."

We learned the alphabet with
silent stubborn teachers
and with errors
through rivulets, pathways, roads and trails
and thus we learned the word "GUINDA"*

Today, August 14, 1984, we teach the alphabet
for the first time with pencil and paper
and we will learn all the words
we have thus far carried in our hearts:
"Victory," "Love."

— Karla, health worker and literacy teacher

*GUINDA: the massive withdrawal of the civilian population in the face of an
army "search and destroy" operation.

QUIENES QUEDARON A MITAD
DEL CAMINO...

Quienes quedaron a mitad del camino
con los ojos hundidos en la niebla.
Quienes miraron por última vez en la noche
o en la semioscuridad de la casita de lata
el vestido triste de la madre,
el semblante enlutado del padre,
la codicia de jardines y chucherías de las hermanas.
Quienes vieron el cielo gris,
los árboles de fuego floreciendo en octubre.
Quienes cantaron en los bares,
pasearon tranquilos un domingo por las calles y los cines.
Quienes tuvieron la oportunidad de ser buenos muchachos
y darle duro a los libros
y darle duro a la vida
y ganarle buena sustancia a la oferta y la demanda.
Quienes pudieron casarse y fundar un lindo hogar
a la orilla del lago más hermoso de la patria.
Quienes salieron una noche con su ropita en una bolsa plástica
y se perdieron para sus familiares.
Quienes abandonaron a la novia
y se internaron en la lluvia de agosto.
Quienes comieron el pan amargo de la frustración de sus
$\qquad\qquad\qquad\qquad\qquad\qquad\qquad$ padres,
quienes liaron cigarrillos de mariguana
y viajaron al norte
quienes gritaron en las manifestaciones
y apedrearon la embajada de Estados Unidos,
quienes conservaron como un pocito limpio
el odio a los explotadores,
quienes se declararon anarquistas, republicanos, demócratas,
marxistas-leninistas,
quienes se levantaron al salir el sol para abrir el surco

THOSE WHO STOPPED
HALFWAY . . .

Those who stopped halfway
with their eyes lost in the fog.
Those who gazed for the last time at night
or in the semi-darkness of the tin shanty
at the sad dress of their mother,
their father's stricken features,
at the greediness of gardens and their sisters' trinkets.
Those who saw the gray sky,
the flame trees flowering in October.
Those who sang in barrooms,
strolled tranquilly one Sunday through streets to the movies.
Those who had the opportunity to be good lads
and work hard at their books
and work hard at life
and make good money out of supply and demand.
Those who could marry and found a lovely home
at the edge of the country's most beautiful lake.
Those who left one night with their clothing in a plastic bag
and were lost forever to their families.
Those who abandoned their girl friends
and plunged into the August rain.
Those who chewed the bitter crusts of their parents'
                                        frustrations,
who rolled marijuana joints
and travelled north,
who shouted in demonstrations
and stoned the U.S. Embassy,
those who conserved like a clear spring
their hatred for the exploiters,
who declared themselves anarchists, republicans,
democrats, Marxist-Lenists,
those who arose at dawn to plow furrows

y ver a la hija del patrón muy linda
pasear a caballo rumbo al río,
quienes tuvieron la desgracia de encontrarse
con guardias nacionales ebrios
y fueron apaleados, heridos o encarcelados,
quienes vieron la violación de su madre
la decapitación de su padre
allá por Chalatenango o Aguilares y pudieron escapar,
quienes abandonaron las tertulias del cafetín,
la universidad, el bachillerato, el tercer ciclo, el sexto grado
y se unieron al vendedor de telas crédito, al campesino,
al lustrador de zapatos, al poblador de tugurios, al huérfano,
al poeta, al hojalatero, al obrero, al mecapalero que tuvo huevos
de desfilar los primeros de mayo en tiempos de Martínez
y se unen por la memoria de los que cayeron en Aguilares,
        Soyapango, Quezaltepeque, San Marcos, Mejicanos,
        Ciudad Delgado, Cuscatancingo y en todos los
        departamentos de El Salvador,
ametrallados, degollados, quebraditos los huesos, castrados,
que les sacaron los ojos
que los despellejaron vivos
que los ahogaron con trapos en la boca
que murieron de una patada en los huevos
que los machetearon y luego los envolvieron en tirrot,
que los quemaron vivos
que los hirvieron en aceite
que les arrancaron los dedos uno por uno
que los hicieron tomar lejía
que les cortaron una vena para desangrarlos.
Por todo eso se unen los de sesenta años y más
con los niños de nueve
y forman en la ciudad y en el campo
los comités populares
las milicias
las guerrillas
el ejército popular.

and watch the pretty boss' daughter
ride by on horseback to the river,
those who had the bad luck
to run into drunken National Guardsmen
and were beaten, wounded or jailed,
those who witnessed the rape of their mother,
the decapitation of their father
in Chalatenango or Aquilares and were able to run for it,
those who abandoned the cafe conversations,
the university, high school, the third cycle, the sixth grade
and joined up with the man who sold cloth bolts on credit,
the peasant, the shoeshine boy, the slum dweller, the orphan,
the poet, the tinsmith, the porter who had the balls
to parade on May Days in the times of Martínez
and they join up in memory of those who fell in Aguilares,
      Soyapango, Quezaltepeque, San Marcos, Mejicanos,
      Ciudad Delgado, Cuscatancingo and in all the
      departments of El Salvador,
machinegunned, throats cut, bones broken, castrated,
eyes gouged out,
skinned alive,
choked with rags in their mouth,
killed by a kick in the balls,
sliced up by machetes and wrapped in gunnysacks,
burned alive,
boiled in oil
those whose fingernails were pulled out one by one,
those who had to swallow lye,
whose veins were slashed so they bled to death.
For all this the 60-year-olds join up
alongside kids of nine
to form in city and countryside
popular committees,
militias,
guerrillas,
the people's army.

Por todo eso hermanos del mundo
luchamos
lucharemos hasta la victoria final.

— José María Cuéllar

For all this, brothers of the world,
we are struggling
and will keep struggling to the final victory.

— José María Cuéllar

ACABO DE PARTIR DE MI MISMO

no soi chema cuéllar
ni soi amigo de nadie
ni tuve una abuela paralytica
ni soy poeta
ni ciudadano
ni nada
me vale un pyto que nadie se acuerde de my
me llevo a san salvador en el volsillo
i hablo con gentes
que no se conocen
ni me conocen
no ymporta si una puerta se cierra en nicaragua
si una muchacha se declara en santiago
sy una paloma vuela por el yan-se
si el mejor libro se está escribiendo en lima
no me importa
estoi vacío
solitario como un abrigo de invierno.

— José María Cuéllar

I JUST WALKED AWAY FROM MYSELF

I'm not chema cuéllar
I'm nobody's friend
I didn't have a paralytic grandmother
and I'm not a poet
nor a citizen
or anything
I don't give a damn if nobody remembers me
I carry myself to san salvador in my pocket
and talk to people who don't know each other
and who don't know me
I don't care if a door slams in nicaragua
if a girl declares her love in santiago
if a dove flies over the yang-tse
if the best book is being written in lima
it doesn't bother me
I'm empty
as alone as a winter overcoat.

— José María Cuéllar

TU VOZ EN MI MENTE

"Entre el tumulto de las otras voces, oí tu voz,
la única que ansiaba".
Tras charrales y cerros
escribo y dibujo
cantos de amor y de guerra
para vos.

Tu voz susurra en el viento
no importa el helicóptero nocturno
que refaguea con lentes infra-rojos
no importan los zancudos y las congas
que producen paludismo
y que día y noche te cobran el descuento de la comida;
no importa mi absurdo temblor de piernas
cuando te tengo enfrente
tus ojos son aquellos mismos
veteranos de la ofensiva de octubre del 81
Chalatenango
tu cuerpo es más diáfano
mas sensible a mis miradas tiernas de gato.
Las caricias y señas se renuevan, amor,
y tus manos,
tus manos son
un
callado testimonio
de un pacto de rebeldía
junto a nuestro pueblo.

— Justo

YOUR VOICE IN MY MIND

"Amidst the tumult of other voices, I heard your voice,
the only one I yearned for."
Amidst shrubtrees and hills
I write and draw
songs of love and war for you.

Your voice whispers in the wind
no matter the nocturnal helicopter
that aims machinegun fire with infra-red lenses
no matter the anophelese mosquitos
that brings bone-breaking malaria
that day and night consumes the food you eat;
no matter the absurd trembling of my legs
when I have you before me
your eyes are the same:
veterans of the October offensive in '81
Chalatenango
your body is more diaphonous
more sensitive to my tender, feline glances.
We renew the caresses and murmurs, love,
and your hands,
your hands are
a
quiet testimony
to a pact of rebellion
made with our people.

— Justo

CUMPLEAÑOS

No es fácil vivir 35 años,
cuando la muerte se pone tan barata
afuera, el oreja que te acecha
busca tus señales: edad, color de piel,
estatura, relaciones familiares.
Adentro, en el frente,
un instante de combate,
una infortunada bomba,
un roquet,
pueden esperarte detrás de los minutos,
a veces, no es fácil
vivir sorteando las tormentas
interiores,
separados de los afectos
armonizando el interés de todos
con los pobres intereses de individuo,
no es fácil venir
amar amando todos las esquinas de los cuartos
todos los atardeceres,
pero a veces sí,
a veces sí cuando sabés que compartís un sol enorme
con todo el universo,
una fuerza irresistible, que derriba fronteras,
que une las voces en un solo himno.
A veces, resulta entonces más que facil.

— Lety, educadora política

BIRTHDAY

It's not easy to live 35 years
when death has become so cheap.
Outside, the informer on your trail
assembles your data: age, color of skin,
height, family relations.
Here at the front
an instant of combat
a hard-luck bomb
a rocket
may await you any minute.
Sometimes it's not easy
to pick your way through inner storms
separated from your affections
harmonizing the interests of all
with petty individual interests
it's not easy to keep on
to love lovingly all corners of all rooms
all the evenings,
but sometimes it is
sometimes when you know you share a huge sun
with all the universe
an irresistible force that demolishes borders
that unites voices in a single hymn,
sometimes it's as easy as can be.

— Lety, political educator

EMBARAZO

Mi niño viene
pequeño transeúnte
a incorporarse a las lluvias de mayo
a las flores abiertas
a las hormigas alegremente locas del invierno.

Mi niño viene,
viajero temporal,
en tiempos de tigres que agonizan
y huracanes que borran las miserias.
Astronauto mudo
siento tu pequeña vida
enviándome cifrados desde tu tibio espacio
y los recojo
para conversar mañana,
cuando tu piel me toque dócilmente,
cuando tu llanto me alegre y me acongoje.

— Lety

PREGNANCY

My baby is coming
tiny wanderer
to mingle with May showers
budding flowers
with winter's joy-crazed ants.

My baby is coming
temporal traveller
in a time of dying tigers
and hurricanes sweeping away misery.
Mute astronaut
I sense your small life
sending me cyphered messages from your warm space
and I receive them
to converse with you tomorrow
when your skin presses mine quietly
and your tears gladden and sadden me.

— Lety

HAY DIAS

Hay días, señor
en que San Salvador se llena
de sombras y de miedo
y sus calles angostas parecen
cementerios cubiertos de ceniza
y creemos que un niño
la muchacha
el amigo
marchan a nuestro lado
y son simples fantasmas
vagas sombras que sueñan
sienten hambre
defecan . . .

Hay días, señor,
en que San Salvador se llena
de estupendas mujeres
que con su movimiento
nos incendian el sexo . . .
El amor es un niño
volando su piscucha
o una pareja
contemplando vitrinas:
el amor se da por canastadas.

Pero hay otros días, señor,
en que San Salvador despierta
de su santa paciencia
y vemos muchachos y obreros
que salen a la calle
a gritar su iracundia
a dejar su protesta
dibujada con sangre sobre el pavimento

THERE ARE DAYS

There are days, sir,
in which San Salvador is filled
with shadows and fear
and its narrow streets resemble
ash-covered cemeteries
and we think that a child
a girl
a friend
walks beside us
and they are simply phantoms
vague shadows that dream
feel hunger
defecate . . .

There are days, sir,
in which San Salvador is filled
with stupendous women
whose movements
inflame our sex . . .
Love is a little boy
flying his kite
or a couple
window-shopping:
there are basketsful of love.

But there are other days, sir,
in which San Salvador arouses
from its saintly patience
and we see youths and workers
take the streets
to shout their anger
to leave their protest
painted in blood on the pavement

a gritar sus canciones
sus poemas
sus sueños . . .

Es entonces, señor,
cuando los enemigos
de los niños sin techo
caminan silenciosos
sombreados por la luna
y golpean las puertas de los ángeles
y los sacan atados a cavar una fosa
donde crecerán flores.

— Jaime Suárez Quemain

to shout their songs
their poems
their dreams . . .

It is then, sir,
when the enemies of roofless children
walk silently
shadowed by the moonlight
and rap on the doors of angels
and take them away, bound, to dig a grave
where flowers will grow.

— Jaime Suárez Quemain

DE NUEVO USTED SEÑOR

. . . y sin embargo usted señor
de respetable estómago
y profunda vocación de comerciante
pese a todos los pesares
y a ese grupo de magnolias ultrajadas
que lleva en la sonrisa
usted señor usted
que un día no remoto
creyó en el mágico poder de la poesía
y tuvo sueños y observó palomas
y jugó a tener el mar
en un viejo rincón abandonado . . .
usted señor que ahora habla
de lo inútil del verso y la verdad
de su panza y ríe con las caricaturas
y se queja de Passolini usted señor
audaz delincuente de etiqueta
que le hace de monstruo
de veleta
de producto del siglo
cuando olvida la samba que le tocan
verá el mundo con ojos de poesía
porque el verso señor
también es para usted
es para todos
él se cuela en las calles
vaga por las vitrinas
cuelga al cuello inocente de los niños
palpita en el rubor
de esas muñecas de hot pants
que usted adquiere a precio módico
se sube a los buses
es amigo de los canillitas

AND YOU AGAIN, GOOD SIR

. . . nevertheless, you, good sir,
with your respectable belly
and your profound mercantile vocation
in spite of everything
including your smile
of mangled magnolia blossoms
you, good sir, you
who not too long ago
believed in the magical power of poetry
and had dreams and watched pigeons
and played at imprisoning the sea
in an old abandoned corner . . .
you, good sir, who now speak
of the uselessness of verse and the truth
of your belly and laugh at the cartoons
and complain about Passolini, you, sir,
audacious delinquent dressed in tuxedo,
pretending to be
weathervane gargoyle,
the century's best-selling product,
when you forget the samba they're playing for you
you will see the world through poetic eyes
because verse, good sir,
is also for you
it is for everyone
it wanders the streets
dawdles before shop windows
hangs from the innocent necks of children
it throbs in the blushes
of those dollies in hot pants
that you acquire at bargain prices
it climbs aboard buses
it is a friend of newsboys

de los obreros
y aunque a veces
muchas veces
le escupe a usted el rostro
el verso a usted quiere salvarlo
llenarle de sonrisas la mirada
inyectarle ternura entre las venas
cobijarle los sueños y ahuyentarle
las pesadillas que lo acosan
el verso señor
desea cambiarle el uniforme
llevarlo a la dry cleaning
y de gratis señor higienizarlo
porque pese a que usted
elude el canto de los pájaros
usted señor usted . . .
puede salvarse.

— Jaime Suárez Quemain

and workers
and though at times
many times
it spits in your face
verse wants to redeem you
fill your gaze with smiles
inject tenderness into your veins
shelter your dreams and ward off
the nightmares that harass you
verse, good sir,
wants to change your uniform
send it off for drycleaning
and disinfect it at no charge
because even though you
elude the song of birds
you, good sir, you . . .
can still be saved.

— Jaime Suárez Quemain

PORQUE CUANDO ESTOY TRISTE
NO ME IMPORTA EL TIEMPO

Daría cualquier cosa por cambiar mi tristeza,
por cambiar la manera complicada
que me arrastra a tus manos,
por ocultar esta forma de mirarte,
este estúpido juego en el que estoy embarcado.
Daría cualquier cosa
por hacer caso omiso a las palabras,
llegar al sicoanálisis y encontrarme dormido,
descubrir que soy triste como un día de lluvia.

      Simplemente me asfixio
      y sangro simplemente.

Porque lloro en las noches
cuando el miedo me envuelve, porque duelen tus ojos
y no basta la angustia
para borrar el agrio temblor que hay en el tiempo.
Porque en este sendero no hay descanso posible
y la meta es una estrella más allá de tu rostro.
Los hombres son fatasmas vagando sobre el polvo
y la vida el camino que nos lleva al olvido.
Las estatuas son sombras tontas prolongaciones
de gente que intentó ser eterna
y terminó en chatarra rodeada de mendigos.

      Simplemente me asfixio
      y tú no lo comprendes
      y si no lo comprendes
      qué más da que me asfixie.

BECAUSE WHEN I'M SAD
THE WEATHER DOESN'T BOTHER ME

I'd give anything to change my sadness,
to change the complex way
that pulls me into your hands,
to hide this way of looking at you,
this stupid game I find myself playing.
I'd give anything
to pay no attention to words,
to be psychoanalyzed and find I'm asleep,
to learn I'm as sad as a rainy day.

     I'm simply asphyxiating
     and I'm bleeding simply.

Because I weep at night
when fear enfolds me, because your eyes wound me
and anguish doesn't suffice
to erase the bitter tremor of time.
Because no rest is possible along the path
and the goal is a star far beyond your face.
Men are phantoms drifting above the dust
and life the road that leads us to forgetting.
Statues are shadows, stupid prolongations
of people who tried to be eternal
and wound up as scrap metal surrounded by beggars.

     I'm simply asphyxiating
     and you don't understand,
     and since you don't understand,
     what difference does it make?

Porque cuando estoy triste no me importa el mal tiempo,
ni la última mordida que me lanzó el amigo,
ni las fauces sangrientas de un idioma extranjero.
Me procupan tus ojos más que el hielo del mundo.
Me preocupas, es todo.
Me preocupas y punto.

— Jaime Suárez Quemain

Because when I'm sad, bad weather doesn't bother me,
nor the latest betrayal by a friend,
nor the bloody jaws of a foreign language.
Your eyes preoccupy me more than the world's ice.
You preoccupy me, that's all.
You preoccupy me, period.

— Jaime Suárez Quemain

LAS CALLES DE SAN SALVADOR

"Siempre hay calles que olvidan sus muertos."
— Benedetti

Las calles de San Salvador jamás serán desmemoriadas.
Saben contar sus muertos
y las sombras para siempre pegadas al asfalto.
Todo lo televisan y lo archivan
con las fechas exactas y sus gritos,
con los cuadernos en busca de sus dueños,
con el hambre asfixiada por tanquetas,
con la incertidumbre del próximo cateo,
con la consigna que se quedó en proyecto,
con el verde muerte de los fanáticos del orden,
con la rabia secreta de un spray clandestino,
con los sueños de sus transeúntes.
Las calles de San Salvador sí que recuerdan sus balazos
y los nombres completos de las víctimas.
Con una memoria de elefante
saben llevar sus estadísticas: el nombre y el lugar,
la angustia y el motivo,
la irracionalidad de los que mandan
y hasta el último grito de los muertos.
De todas sus paredes se desprenden mensajes
que llenan la ciudad de rebeldía,
que se meten en todos los hogares
formando un ventarrón de esperanzas libertarias.
Las calles de San Salvador jamás serán desmemoriadas
porque un día hablarán serenamente justicieras,
una por una hablarán
y no habrá quien eluda sus miradas.
Espontáneas se ofrecerán para servir de paredones,
no en plan de venganza,

THE STREETS OF SAN SALVADOR

"There are always streets that forget their dead."
— Benedetti

The streets of San Salvador will never disremember.
They know how to count their dead
and the shadows forever etched in asphalt.
They videotape and file everything,
with the exact dates and the screams,
with the notebooks in search of owners,
with hunger asphyxiated by tanks,
with the uncertainty as to the next police break-in,
with the slogan only half-sketched,
with the olive green death of the fanatics of order,
with the secret rage of a clandestine spray can,
with the daydreams of the passersby.
The streets of San Salvador remember every gunshot
and the complete names of the victims.
They keep statistics
with an elephant's memory: the name and place,
the anguish and the motive,
the irrationality of those in charge
and even the last scream of the dying.
Messages drip from all their walls
filling the city with rebellion,
seeping into all the homes,
forming gusts of libertarian hopes.
The streets of San Salvador will never disremember
because one day they shall speak out as serene justice,
one by one they shall speak
and no one will elude their gazes.
Spontaneously they will offer themselves as execution walls,
not in thirst of vengeance,

sino para limpiar con justicia obrera
el terreno donde construiremos el mañana.

-Jaime Suárez Quemain

but simply to clear with worker's justice
the terrain where we will erect our tomorrow.

— Jaime Suárez Quemain.

CLARIBEL ALEGRÍA was born on May 12, 1924 in Estelí, Nicaragua, but considers herself Salvadoran since she moved early in her life to Santa Ana, El Salvador where she grew up. She has become a major voice in the struggle for liberation in El Salvador, and in Central America. She has published 10 volumes of poetry, 3 short novels and a book of children's stories in Spanish, and translations of her work have been published in France, Holland, England and the United States. Her book, *Sobrevivo*, won the 1978 Casa de las Américas Prize for poetry.

DARWIN J. FLAKOLL was born on February 20, 1923 in Wendte, South Dakota. He served as a deck officer aboard destroyers during World War II. Following the war, he was Washington correspondent for a number of western newspapers and assistant bureau manager of Western Reporters News Agency before moving to Mexico City in 1950 where he worked as managing editor of the Mexico City Daily News. In 1953, at the beginning of his collaborative work with Claribel Alegría, Flakoll served as second secretary at the embassies in Montevideo and Buenos Aires before returning to newspaper work as a foreign correspondent for International Feature Service. Darwin Flakoll died at his home in Managua in 1995.

Claribel Alegría and Darwin J. Flakoll met during their studies at George Washington University and subsequently got married. They moved to Mallorca in 1966, and then to Managua, Nicaragua in 1979. Over the years, they have collaborated on 9 books of testimony, Latin American history and literary anthologies.

Related Salvadoran titles
available from Curbstone Press

ASHES OF IZALCO, a novel by Claribel Alegría and Darwin J. Flakoll, trans. by Darwin J. Flakoll. A love story which unfolds during the bloody events of 1932, when 30,000 Indians and peasants were massacred in Izalco, El Salvador.

$17.95cl   ISBN 0-915306-83-2 / $12.95pa   ISBN 0-915306-84-0

CLANDESTINE POEMS / POEMAS CLANDESTINOS by Roque Dalton; translated by Jack Hirschman. Written just before his assassination, these poems deliver Dalton's political insights into the situation in El Salvador with biting humor, strength, and tenderness.

$12.95pa   0-915306-91-3

LITTLE RED RIDING HOOD IN THE RED LIGHT DISTRICT, a novel by Manlio Argueta; trans. by Ed Hood. A story of two young lovers in a time of political upheaval, evoking characters and themes from the classic fairy tale within a wartime environment. "...charmingly elusive political romance...through the voices of his characters, Argueta portrays the aspirations of an entire generation." —*Publishers Weekly*

$14.95pa   1-880684-32-2

MIGUEL MARMOL, by Roque Dalton; trans. by Richard Schaaf. Long considered a classic testimony throughout Latin America, Miguel Marmol gives a detailed account of Salvadoran history while telling the interesting and sometimes humorous story of one man's life.

$19.95cl   ISBN 0-915306-68-9 / $12.95pa   ISBN 0-915306-67-0

MATANZA, by Thomas P. Anderson. Newly revised and available for the first time in paperback, Thomas Anderson's 1971 landmark study of the 1932 revolt and subsequent government massacre in El Salvador is the seminal work on the origins of the current social conflict in that country.

$14.95pa   ISBN 1-880684-04-7

A PLACE CALLED MILAGRO DE LA PAZ, a novel by Manlio Argueta; trans. by Michael Miller. This novel tells the story of the courage and strength of a single mother and her daughter who must overcome the murder of the mother's older daughter and survive bitter poverty. The tiny family bravely preserves traditional values in spite of fear and repression. "It takes a master to turn a story of pain and tragedy into a thing of beauty. But then Manlio Argueta is a proven master of words."—Beatriz Terrazas, *Dallas Morning News*

$14.95pa   1-880684-68-3

REBEL RADIO: The story of El Salvador's Radio Venceremos, by José Ignacio López Vigil; trans. by Mark Fried. During El Salvador's civil war, a clandestine radio station, Radio Venceremos, operated in-country by broadcasting in secret mountain locations, constantly on the run from the army. *Rebel Radio* is the heroic and human inside story of this endeavor, adventure interwoven with the embattled modern history of Central America.

$19.95cl   ISBN 1-890684-21-17   incl. photos & maps

SMALL HOURS OF THE NIGHT, poetry by Roque Dalton; edited by Hardie St. Martin. Here for the first time in English is a collection that reveals the full range of his poetic talent. "This selection...crackles with energy, anger, and desire. Dalton makes the suffering and exhaustion of the poor and the imprisoned tangible..."—*Minneapolis Star Tribune*

$14.95pa   1-880684-35-7

FOR MORE INFORMATION, SEND A REQUEST TO:
Curbstone Press, 321 Jackson St., Willimantic, CT 06226
or visit us at http://www.curbstone.org

CURBSTONE PRESS, INC.

is a nonprofit publishing house dedicated to literature that reflects a commitment to social change, with an emphasis on contemporary writing from Latino, Latin American and Vietnamese cultures. Curbstone presents writers who give voice to the unheard in a language that goes beyond denunciation to celebrate, honor and teach. Curbstone builds bridges between its writers and the public – from inner-city to rural areas, colleges to community centers, children to adults. Curbstone seeks out the highest aesthetic expression of the dedication to human rights and intercultural understanding: poetry, testimonies, novels, stories, children's books.

This mission requires more than just producing books. It requires ensuring that as many people as possible learn about these books and read them. To achieve this, a large portion of Curbstone's schedule is dedicated to arranging tours and programs for its authors, working with public school and university teachers to enrich curricula, reaching out to underserved audiences by donating books and conducting readings and community programs, and promoting discussion in the media. It is only through these combined efforts that literature can truly make a difference.

Curbstone Press, like all nonprofit presses, depends on the support of individuals, foundations, and government agencies to bring you, the reader, works of literary merit and social significance which might not find a place in profit-driven publishing channels, and to bring the authors and their books into communities across the country. Our sincere thanks to the following foundations, and government agencies who support this endeavor: Connecticut Commission on the Arts, Connecticut Humanities Council, Daphne Seybolt Culpeper Foundation, Fisher Foundation, Greater Hartford Arts Council, Hartford Courant Foundation, J. M. Kaplan Fund, Eric Mathieu King Fund, Lannan Foundation, John D. and Catherine T. MacArthur Foundation, National Endowment for the Arts, Open Society Institute, Puffin Foundation, and the Woodrow Wilson National Fellowship Foundation.

Please help to support Curbstone's efforts to present the diverse voices and views that make our culture richer. Tax-deductible donations can be made by check or credit card to:
Curbstone Press, 321 Jackson Street, Willimantic, CT 06226
phone: (860) 423-5110   fax: (860) 423-9242